Tomtom
The baby loves you

Story Assist. Prof. Arunnit Boonrod and Nicole Briann Luloff **Illustration** Wenny Stefanie **Special consultant** Donlaya Prasathaporn (Pediatrician) and Thitima Sirikangwalkul **Editor** Assist. Prof. Artit Boonrod and Assist. Prof. Arunnit Boonrod **Assistant editor** Jira Chainuwat
Published by BaanSiTao, Khonkaen, Thailand **E-mail** BaanSiTao@gmail.com **Facebook and Line ID** BaanSiTao

In my mommy's tummy, something is moving.
Oh, it's the baby! She just loves kicking.

If she grasps you tight at one-month-old, the
baby loves you and she wants you to know.

Your little baby, now she's two months.
Smiling at you means she loves you a whole
bunch.

At three months,
she's always looking for you.
She wants you near,
to play and laugh, too.

Babbling four-month-old baby, so adorable.
Her voice is lovely, but not understandable.

Five months and just like you,
she makes silly faces.
She's copying you because you are
the best.

Six months.

Giving and passing things to you,
to show her love.
You are the best big brother she
could ever think of.

Seven months.

She is having fun rolling over and often bumps her head.

You have to stick tight or she might fall from the bed.

Eight months.

Crawling so fast, yes, she can do it!

She wants to follow you

and is determined to do it.

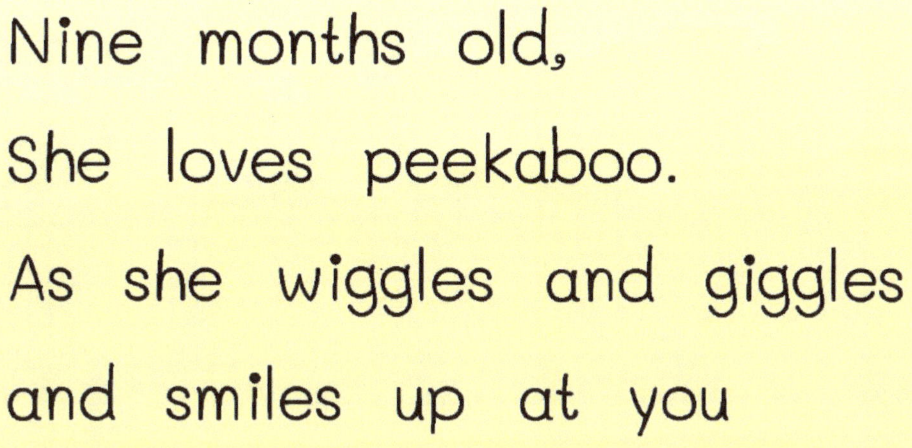

Nine months old,
She loves peekaboo.
As she wiggles and giggles
and smiles up at you

At 10 months,
she begins to wobble and stand.
She is very sure of herself
with her big brother holding her hand

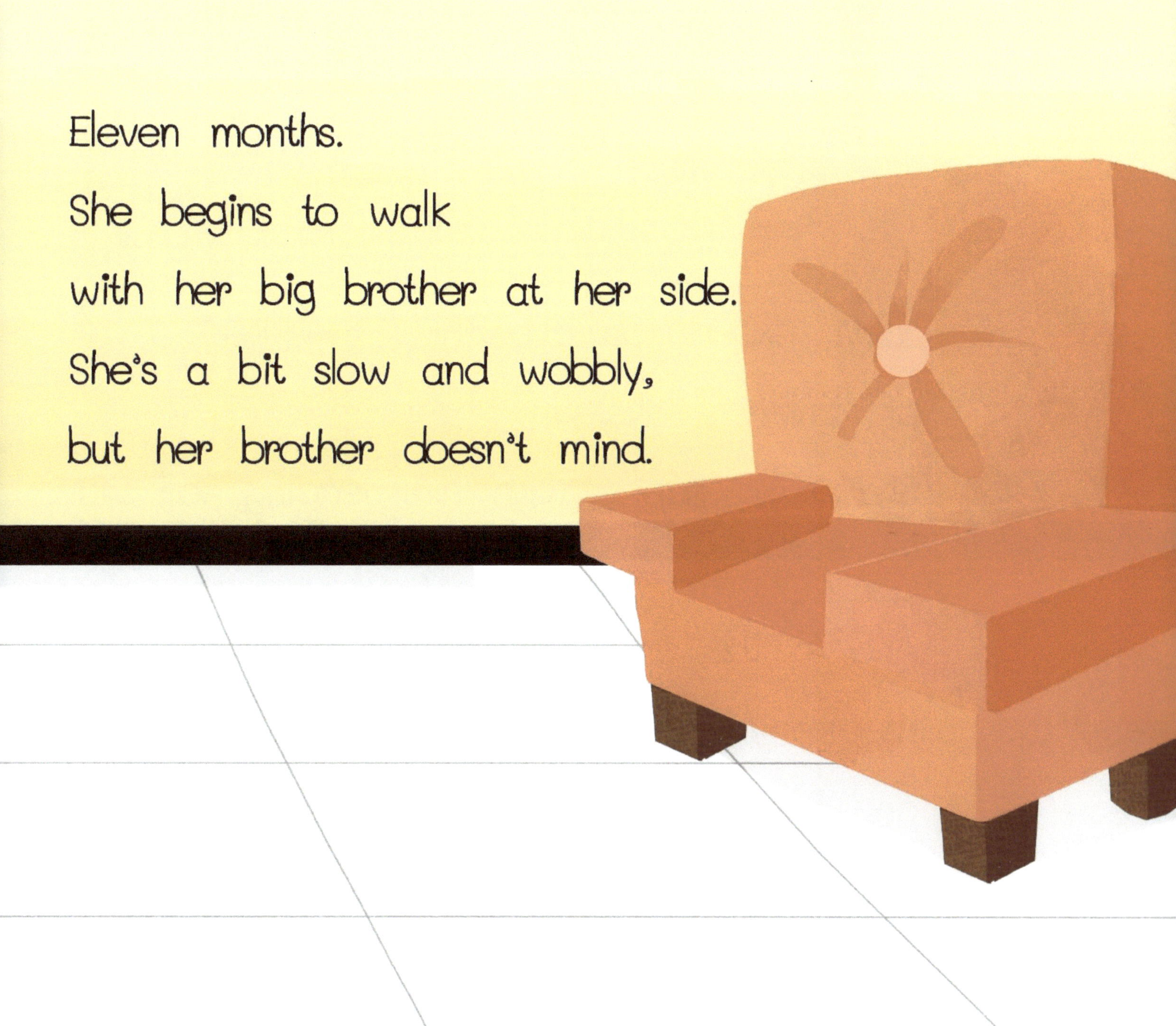

Eleven months.
She begins to walk
with her big brother at her side.
She's a bit slow and wobbly,
but her brother doesn't mind.

As a one-year-old, she starts to run.
Sometimes she falls, but that's okay.
Life is so much fun.

"Let's experience everything together",
big brother says,
She is so happy with him leading the way.

And in the end, one thing's for sure,
the baby loves her brother,
and her brother loves her.

Developmental milestones for 1-year-olds

1 month

- 🏃 Can lift head when laying on tummy momentarily.
- ✋ Eye movement follow objects.
- 👥 Look at faces.
- 💬 Cry.
- 👂 React to sound.

2 months

- 🏃 Can lift head when laying on tummy.
- ✋ Starts recognizing people.
- 👥 Begins to smile.
- 💬 Make cooing sounds
- 👂 Responses to sound with a blink.

3-4 months

- 🏃 Pushes up to elbows, holds head steady.
- ✋ Looks and reaches for things.
- 👥 Shows affection.
- 💬 Babbles.
- 👂 Turns to sound.

5-6 months

- 🏃 Rolls over in both directions.
- ✋ Grabs and passes things.
- 👥 Laughs when play, especially with parents.
- 💬 Makes more sounds.
- 👂 Reponses to his name.

7-8 months

- 🏃 Sits without support.
- ✋ Passes thinks between hands.
- 👥 Likes to play cover/uncover face with blanket.
- 💬 Copies simple sounds.
- 👂 Looks where parents point.

9-10 months

- 🏃 Pulls to stand, to sit or crawls.
- ✋ Uses fingers to point.
- 👥 Loves peekaboo. Waves bye-bye.
- 💬 Makes more sounds like "mama" or "dada".
- 👂 Reponses to simple tasks.

11-12 months

- 🏃 Stand momentarily
- ✋ Gives things when ask
- 👥 Copies gestures
- 💬 Makes sound with different tones
- 👂 Understands one syllable words and responds to simple requests.

Five main areas of development

- 🏃 Gross motor skill development.
- ✋ Fine motor skill development.
- 👥 Social and emotional development.
- 💬 Speech and language development.
- 👂 Cognitive development.